Japanese Ghost Stories

Lafcadio Hearn

Level 3

Retold by Jane Rollason

Series Editors: Andy Hopkins and Jocelyn Potter

Pearson Education Limited
Edinburgh Gate, Harlow,
Essex CM20 2JE, England
and Associated Companies throughout the world.

ISBN: 9781292110370

This edition first published by Pearson Education Ltd 2008

1 3 5 7 9 10 8 6 4 2

Text copyright © Pearson Education Ltd 2008
Illustrations by Yuko Aoki
The author has asserted her moral right in accordance with the
Copyright Designs and Patents Act 1988

Set in 11/13pt A. Garamond
Printed in China
SWTC/01

Produced for the Publishers by AC Estudio Editorial S.L.

Published by Pearson Education Ltd

Acknowledgements
We are grateful to the following for permission to reproduce photographs:
Mary Evans Picture Library: Harpers Magazine 72tr

*Every effort has been made to trace the copyright holders and we apologise in advance for any unintentional omissions.
We would be pleased to insert the appropriate acknowledgement in any subsequent edition of this publication.*

For a complete list of the titles available in the Pearson English Active Readers series, visit www.pearsonenglishactivereaders.com.
Alternatively, write to your local Pearson Education office or to
Pearson English Readers Marketing Department, Pearson Education, Edinburgh Gate, Harlow, Essex CM20 2JE, England.

Contents

	Activities 1	iv
Story 1	The Blind Musician Activities 2	1 12
Story 2	The Fortune-Teller's Story	14
Story 3	The Great Fire of the Purple Robe	17
Story 4	The Travelling Priest and the Dead Body Activities 3	19 24
Story 5	Miyata's Dream	26
Story 6	A Dead Secret	31
Story 7	You Can't Trick a Samurai Activities 4	34 36
Story 8	The Mirror and the Bell	38
Story 9	The Woman in White Activities 5	43 48
Story 10	The Bouncing Heads	50
Story 11	The Samurai and the Tree Activities 6	58 60
Story 12	Mujina	62
Story 13	The Hungry Hunter	64
Story 14	The Promise	66
Story 15	The Mountain	69
	Talk about it Write about it Project: A Two-Minute Ghost Play	72 73 74

1.1 What's the book about?

1 Read about the stories on the back of the book. Then discuss the picture on the front cover.

    a Where are these stories from?

    b What do you think the cover story is about?

2 These words are all important in the stories. Check their meanings at the bottom of pages 1 and 2. Then put the right forms of the words in the story below.

blind   ghost   haunt   pray   priest   spirit   temple

A man was walking through a dark forest when, suddenly, he saw an old stone ᵃ .... There was a stone buddha in the wall. A ᵇ .... was on his knees, ᶜ .... to the buddha. The man called the priest and the priest turned to him. The man saw that his eyes were closed. He was ᵈ .... The man was afraid. He felt that there were ᵉ .... dancing in the air around him. Was the temple ᶠ ....? He looked behind him. There were only dark trees. He turned back. The priest was gone. He wasn't a priest – he was a ᵍ ....! The man screamed and ran back into the forest.

3 Discuss these questions.

    a You are in an old house with a friend. You go upstairs and see strange lights. Suddenly, there is a loud noise. What will you do?

    b Do you believe in ghosts? Have you ever seen one? Tell the story.

1.2 What happens first?

Read the words in *italics* on page 1, opposite, and look at the picture. What do you think? Tick (✓) the best answers.

1 The listeners are listening to

    a ☐ a ghost story.   **b** ☐ the story of a big fight.

2 They are crying wildly because

    a ☐ the story is so sad.   **b** ☐ they are going to die.

The Blind Musician

All the listeners cried out together – a long, long cry of pain.
They cried loudly and wildly and the blind man was frightened.

More than 700 years ago there was a great fight at sea at a place called Dan-no-ura. It was the last great fight between two peoples – the Heiké and the Genji. All the Heiké fighters died there with their women and children, and their child **emperor**. His name was Antoku Tennō. And the Heiké **ghost**s have **haunt**ed that coast since that time.

The Heiké ghosts are quieter these days, but in earlier times they were a danger to ships. Ghostly lights circled around ships in the night as the **spirit**s tried to pull them down under the water. They watched for swimmers and tried to pull them down too.

In a town on that coast – Akamagaséki – the people of the town built a Buddhist **temple** to try to please the Heiké spirits. The temple was called Amidaji. They built a garden for the dead too, near the beach. They put up

emperor /'empərə/ (n) the head of government of a country, or a number of countries; these lands are his *empire*
ghost /gəʊst/ (n) the part of a person that lives after death. *Ghostly* places are visited by ghosts.
haunt /hɔːnt/ (v) to visit a place often (used of ghosts and spirits)
spirit /'spɪrɪt/ (n) the part of a person that is believed to live after death
temple /'tempəl/ (n) a place where people practise their religion

stones with the names of the child emperor and his great followers. A Buddhist **priest** said **prayer**s for the spirits of the dead. After that, the Heiké were less trouble. But they did strange things at times; something was still worrying them.

At that time there lived a young **blind** man named Hōïchi. He was famous for **perform**ing poems and playing the *biwa**. He learned both skills as a child, and he soon performed better than his teachers.

Hōïchi grew up and became a professional *biwa* player, and his most famous performance was the history of the Heiké and the Genji. When he sang the song of Dan-no-ura, even the bad spirits cried.

At first Hōïchi was very poor. Then he found a good friend at the Amidaji temple. The priest of the temple loved poems and music, and he often asked Hōïchi to perform for him. He thought young Hōïchi had wonderful skills. The priest invited Hōïchi to live at the temple, and Hōïchi accepted gratefully. In

* *biwa*: you make music with this

priest /priːst/ (n) the officer of a temple
pray /preɪ/ (v) to ask the Buddha for help. A *prayer* is the words that you say.
blind /blaɪnd/ (adj) unable to see
perform /pəˈfɔːm/ (v) to dance, sing or act in front of other people; to do

return for food and a bed, Hōïchi only had to perform on two or three evenings each week.

One summer night, the priest was called away. His assistant went with him and Hōïchi was left alone in the temple. It was a hot night and the blind man was too warm in his bedroom.

Behind his room was a small garden. Hōïchi waited for the priest there and practised the *biwa*. Midnight passed and the priest did not return. But Hōïchi stayed outside.

At last he heard some footsteps at the back gate. They came nearer. Somebody crossed the little garden and stopped in front of Hōïchi … but it was not the priest.

'Hōïchi!' A deep, angry voice called the blind man's name. It was the voice of a *samurai**.

* *samurai*: a class of Japanese soldiers, seen as upper class from the late 1500s

Hōïchi was very surprised and frightened, and at first he did not answer. 'Hōïchi!'

'Yes?' the blind man answered this time. 'I cannot see. I do not know who is calling me.'

'There is nothing to fear,' said the stranger more quietly. 'I have a message for you from my **lord**. My lord is a man of very high class, and he is now staying in Akamagaséki, with many followers. He came to see where the great sea fight of Dan-no-ura took place. And now he wants to hear the story of the fight. He has heard of your skill and he is waiting for you. Bring your *biwa* and come with me.'

Hōïchi put on his shoes and picked up his *biwa*. He went away with the stranger. The stranger guided him carefully. Hōïchi could hear that he wore metal.

'He is probably a palace guard,' thought Hōïchi, and he began to feel happier. 'I am in luck. His lord is an important man.'

They walked for some time. Hōïchi had to walk very fast to stay with him. And then the *samurai* stopped outside a large gateway. Hōïchi was surprised. He could not remember a large gateway in that part of the town; only the main gate of the Amidaji temple.

'*Kaimon*!*' shouted the *samurai*.

Hōïchi jumped. Then he heard the gates opening.

They crossed a garden and stopped in front of another entrance. Then the *samurai* cried in a loud voice, 'I have brought Hōïchi.'

Suddenly there were many sounds: feet hurrying, doors opening, women's voices. Hōïchi knew he was in the house of a lord, but which lord and where? He did not have much time to think. He climbed some stone steps. He was told to leave his shoes on the last step. Then a woman's hand guided him across smooth wooden floors.

At last they came into the middle of a great room. Hōïchi felt there were many people in the room. He could hear many quiet voices, all talking together. Their speech was the speech of a lord's court.

'Do not be afraid, Hōïchi,' said a woman's voice. 'Please make yourself comfortable here on the floor.'

Hōïchi sat down and prepared his *biwa*.

'My lord requests you to perform the history of the Heiké, in speech and music,' said the woman.

The story was long. Many nights were needed for it. Hōïchi bravely asked a question. 'As the history of the Heiké is long, which part of it shall I now perform?'

---

* *Kaimon!*: a *samurai*'s call to the guards when he wanted to pass through his lord's gate

lord /lɔːd/ (n) a very important person with many soldiers and a lot of land

The woman answered, 'Tell the story of the great fight of Dan-no-ura, because that is the saddest part.'

Then Hōïchi lifted up his voice and began his story. He made his *biwa* sound like great fighting ships on the waves and the crashing of metal on wood. In his story, men fought and cried, and bodies were thrown into the sea. The water turned red with their blood.

Voices around Hōïchi talked of his skill: 'What a wonderful artist!' 'I have never heard playing like this!' 'No other singer in the empire is as good as Hōïchi.' These words made Hōïchi feel braver. He played and sang better than before. But then he came to the deaths of the fair women and helpless children – and the death of the child emperor. All the listeners cried out together – a long, long cry of pain. They cried loudly and wildly and the blind man was frightened. Slowly the sounds died away until the great room was quiet again.

Then the woman spoke. 'We heard that you played the *biwa* well,' she said. 'We heard that you performed poems beautifully. But we did not know that anyone could perform like this. You have taken us to the heart of the great fight of Dan-no-ura tonight. Our lord is very pleased. He wants you to perform again tomorrow night and for the next six nights. After that, he will probably make his return journey. Tomorrow night the palace guard will come for you again.

'There is one more thing. No one knows that our lord has travelled here. His journey here is secret. Please do not tell anyone about your visits here. … You are now free to go back to your temple.'

Hōïchi thanked the speaker, and a woman's hand guided him back to the entrance. The same *samurai* waited there to take him home. He left Hōïchi in the small garden behind his room.

It was almost daylight when Hōïchi returned. Nobody saw him go and nobody saw him come back. The priest returned late. He imagined that Hōïchi was asleep in his room. Hōïchi slept a little during the day and said nothing about his strange adventure.

In the middle of the next night, the *samurai* again came for him and took him back to the great room. Hōïchi performed another part of the history of the Heiké. His second performance was as successful as his first. But during this second visit, the priest at the Amidaji temple discovered that Hōïchi was not there.

The next morning, the priest called Hōïchi to see him.

'We were very worried about you, friend Hōïchi. You are blind! It is very dangerous for you to go out alone and so late. Why didn't you tell us? I can always send someone with you. And where did you go?'

'I am very sorry, kind friend!' Hōïchi answered carefully. 'I had some private business.' He said no more.

The priest was surprised, but not angry. Hōïchi was acting strangely. Perhaps some bad spirits were at work here. He did not ask any more questions. But privately he asked his temple assistants to watch Hōïchi. He asked them to follow Hōïchi if he left the temple after dark again.

That night, the assistants saw Hōïchi leave the temple. They immediately lit their lights and followed him. But it was a rainy night, and very dark. Before they reached the roadway, Hōïchi disappeared.

'How can he walk so fast?' they asked. 'He is blind and there are many holes in the road.'

The men hurried through the streets. They asked at every house, but nobody had any news of Hōïchi. At last they turned to go home. They were returning to the temple along the beach when they suddenly heard a *biwa*. The sounds came from the garden of the dead next to the temple.

A few ghostly fires seemed to hang in the blackness above the stones. The men ran to the place with their lights; and there they found Hōïchi. He was sitting alone in the rain in front of a large stone. The name of Antoku Tenno was on the stone. Hōïchi was telling the story of the great fight of Dan-no-ura. And behind him, around him and above him, the *Oni-bi** hung over the stones.

'Hōïchi *San**! Hōïchi *San!*' cried the temple assistants. 'These are bad spirits! … Hōïchi *San!*'

But the blind man did not seem to hear. He played his *biwa* more and more wildly. He was almost screaming the poem. They caught his clothes; they shouted in his ear, 'Hōïchi *San!* Hōïchi *San!* Come home with us immediately!' Hōïchi spoke to them angrily. 'Do not speak to me so rudely, in front of these important listeners.'

* *Oni-bi*: the bad spirit fires of the dead
* *San*: a word for Sir, placed after a person's name

The assistants looked at Hōïchi and at his 'listeners' and then started to laugh. They were sure that there were spirits all around him. They pulled him to his feet and hurried back to the temple with him. They gave him dry clothes and a hot drink, and then the priest asked for a full explanation.

Hōïchi said nothing at first. But then he understood that the priest was angry with him. He decided to speak. He told the story from the first visit of the *samurai*.

The priest said, 'Hōïchi, my poor friend, you are now in great danger! I am sorry that you did not tell me all this before! Your wonderful skill in music has brought you into strange trouble. You must know now that you have not visited

a house. You passed the night in the place of the dead. You were sitting in front of Antoku Tenno's stone when we found you. Everything was in your imagination; nothing was real, except the calling of the dead. You did what they asked. Now you are in trouble. Next time, they will pull you to pieces.'

The priest had business away from the temple again that evening. He could not stay with Hōïchi.

'Before I go,' he said to Hōïchi, 'we will protect your body. We will write Buddhist prayers on it.'

Before the sun went down, the priest and his assistant took off Hōïchi's clothes. They painted the prayers all over his body, his head, face and neck, his legs and arms, his hands and feet. After that, the priest told Hōïchi what to do.

'Tonight, as soon as I go away, you must wait in your small garden. When the *samurai* calls you, do not answer. Do not move. Say nothing. If you move, he will pull you to pieces. Do not be frightened. Do not call for help – because no help can save you. Do exactly as I tell you. Then the danger will pass. You will have nothing more to fear.'

After dark, the priest and his assistant went away. Hōïchi sat in the small garden and put his *biwa* on the ground next to him. For hours he sat and did not move.

Then he heard footsteps coming from the roadway. The footsteps passed the gate and crossed the small garden. They stopped not far from Hōïchi.

'Hōïchi!' called the deep voice. But the blind man did not answer.

Hōïchi!' called the voice a second time, more angrily. Then it called a third time, now very angrily, 'Hōïchi!'

Hōïchi did not move.

'No answer? Where is he?'

The footsteps came right up to the blind *biwa* player. For a long minute, there was silence. Hōïchi's heart raced inside his body.

At last the deep voice spoke close to Hōïchi. 'Here is the *biwa*. But where is the *biwa* player? I see … only two ears! So that explains why he did not answer. He has no mouth to answer with. There is nothing left of him except his ears … I will take those ears to my lord. He will believe me then.'

Fingers closed on Hōïchi's ears and pulled hard. They pulled Hōïchi's ears off his head! The pain was sharp and terrible, but Hōïchi did not make a sound. The heavy footsteps went back across the garden, out onto the roadway and disappeared. Hōïchi felt thick, warm blood on both sides of his head, but he did not lift his hands …

Before the sun came up, the priest returned. He ran to the small garden behind Hōïchi's room, stepped on something wet and fell. It was blood! He gave a terrible cry but then saw Hōïchi. Hōïchi was still sitting in the same place. Blood ran slowly and thickly from the holes in the sides of his head.

'My poor Hōïchi!' cried the priest. 'What is this? You are hurt!'

When he heard his friend's voice, the blind man felt safe at last. Tears poured down his face and he told the priest about his adventure of the night.

10

'Poor, poor Hōïchi!' said the priest. 'This is all because of me! We wrote Buddhist prayers all over your body, except on your ears! That was my assistant's job and I did not check his work. It was very, very wrong of me! Well, it is too late now. We must try to stop the pain quickly. Smile, my friend! The danger is over. Your ghostly visitors will never trouble you again.'

Hōïchi was soon better, with the help of a good doctor. The story of his strange adventure travelled all over the country, and made him famous. Many important people came to Akamagaséki to hear his performances. They gave him large presents of money and he became very rich. From the time of his adventure, he had a new name: Hōïchi-No-Ears!

Today you can still see and hear many strange things along that coast. You can find strange fish – fish with Heiké faces on their backs. People say these are the spirits of Heiké *samurai*. And on dark nights, thousands of ghostly fires seem to hang over the waves – pale lights, called *Oni-bi* by the fishermen. When the winds are strong, you can hear terrible noises from the sea, like the sound of men killing men.

2.1 Were you right?

Look back at Activity 1.2 on page iv. Then tick (✓) the right sentences below. Put a cross (✗) next to the sentences that are wrong.

1 ☐ The Heiké ghosts were a danger to ships and swimmers before the temple at Akamagaséki was built.

2 ☐ Hōïchi tells stories in words and music.

3 ☐ The *samurai* stops at a large gateway. Hōïchi knows where he is.

4 ☐ The listeners are not afraid of death because they are already dead.

5 ☐ The priest paints prayers on every part of Hōïchi's body.

6 ☐ The prayers hide Hōïchi's body from the *samurai* … except his ears.

2.2 What more did you learn?

Match the words below with a picture of a possible speaker. Write the letters, A–E.

1 ☐ 'Have you seen Hōïchi? Did he come this way?'

2 ☐ 'Are you sure you painted every part of him?'

3 ☐ 'We must hear the end of the story and then we can rest.'

4 ☐ 'I can still hear. And I am happy to be alive!'

5 ☐ 'This is all there was – a pair of ears.'

Language in use

Look at the sentence on the right. Then complete the sentences below in the same way. Choose two verbs for each sentence from the box below.

> The priest **invited** Hōïchi **to live** at the temple.

| tell | ask | want | follow | pay | perform | play | say | tell | watch |

1 The *samurai* .... Hōïchi .... him.

2 The lord .... Hōïchi .... the story of Dan-no-ura.

3 The priest .... his temple assistants .... Hōïchi.

4 The priest .... Hōïchi .... nothing to the *samurai*.

5 Important people .... Hōïchi .... the *biwa*.

What happens next?

1 The next story is about a fortune-teller. Read the words in *italics* on page 14 and check the meanings of new words. Then look at the picture on page 15. What do you think is going to happen in this story? Make notes.

Notes

2 Tell your fortune. What will happen to you in the future?

....

....

The Fortune-Teller's Story

Shōko Setsu looked sadly at the broken cup, and was sorry for his angry feelings. Then he looked more closely at it.

This is the story of a **fortune**-teller who really believed in fortune-telling. As a young man, he was a *samurai* for a rich *daimyō**. But then hard times came. Like thousands of other *samurai*, he suddenly had no work. So he learned to be a fortune-teller. He travelled on foot from town to town and he was quite successful as a fortune-teller. There were two main reasons for this. First, he really believed what he told people. Second, he was a kind and quiet man, and people wanted to believe him.

He used the Chinese way of telling fortunes – the *I-Ching** He learned to read the book of the *I-Ching* quite well, but he was not always right.

'When a skilled fortune-teller uses the *I-Ching*,' he told his customers, 'it is never wrong. *I* sometimes make mistakes, but only because I cannot always read the signs correctly.'

Often he told fortunes correctly and then his customers became afraid of him. We all believe a little in fortune-telling. We cannot help it even if we are followers of science. When something strange happens, we quickly forget science. Then we start to believe in luck.

The fortune-teller grew older, but he continued to travel all through the year, even in the colder months. He loved his free life. He learned many things and heard many stories all over the country. He had one favourite story that he often told:

'This story is about a famous Chinese fortune-teller called Shōko Setsu. He was very good and very clever. He used the *I-Ching*. He was given a very important position at the emperor's court. But he only wanted to study and he gave up the position. For many years he lived alone in a hut in the mountains. He studied without a fire in the winter. He had no paper, so he wrote his thoughts on the wall of his room. When he slept, he rested his head on a stone.

'One hot summer's day, he felt sleepy and hot. He took a drink of water and put his cup next to his stone. Then he lay down on the floor of his hut. He was just falling asleep when something ran across his face. He was angry, picked up his cup and threw it at the animal. But the animal escaped, and the cup was

---

* *daimyō*: an important land-owner in Japan from about 1000 to 1900
* *I-Ching*: an old Chinese fortune-telling book

fortune /ˈfɔːtʃən/ (n) our future; a large amount of money

broken. Shōko Setsu looked sadly at the broken cup, and was sorry for his angry feelings. Then he looked more closely at it. There were seventeen Chinese **character**s along the line of the break. This, he thought, was very strange. Were they written before the cup was hardened in the oven? This is what they said:

"In the Year of the Horse, in the fourth month, on the seventeenth day, at the fourteenth hour, this cup will fly across a hut in the mountains and break."

character /ˈkærɪktə/ (n) used in writing, like a letter

'This *was* the fourteenth hour of the seventeenth day of the fourth month of the Year of the Horse, so Shōko Setsu was very surprised. He looked at the pieces of the cup again and found the name of its maker. He left his hut immediately and hurried to the neighbouring town. There he found the maker's workplace. He showed him the cup and asked about its history.

'The maker looked carefully at the pieces, and then said, "This cup was made here, but the characters were written by an old man. He was a fortune-teller and he wanted to write on the cup before I put it in the oven."

'"Do you know where he lives?" asked Shōko Setsu.

'"His house is not far from here. I can show you the way, but I do not know his name."

'When Shōko Setsu arrived at the house, he asked to see the old man. A student invited him into a room where five or six other young men were studying. One of the young men spoke to Shōko Setsu.

'"We are very sorry to tell you that our teacher died a few days ago. But we are waiting for you. He knew that you would come to this house at this hour on this day. Your name is Shōko Setsu. Our teacher left this book for you. Here – please accept it."

'Shōko Setsu was very surprised and very pleased. There was no other book like this, he knew, and it held many secrets about fortune-telling. He thanked the young men and returned to his hut in the mountains. He decided to test the book and he asked it about his own future. The book sent him to a corner of the hut. Great luck was waiting for him there, it said. And under the earth in the corner of his little hut, he found a pot of gold.'

Our old Japanese fortune-teller was not as lucky as Shōko Setsu. In his sixtieth year, he left this world. It was winter and he was following a path through some mountains. A snowstorm came up and he lost his way. Many days later, he was found. He was standing at the foot of a tall tree, with his little bag on his back. His arms hung across his body and his eyes were closed. He was frozen. He probably fell asleep while he was waiting for the end of the storm.

When people heard of his strange death, they remembered the old Japanese saying: 'The fortune-teller cannot see his own future.'

The Great Fire of the Purple Robe

The priest was able to sell the robe at a good price. It was an expensive robe,
and the dead girl's tears did not show.

About 250 years ago, a rich wine-seller lived in Tokyo, the city of the *shōgun**. One day, the wine-seller and his family were at their local temple. It was a holiday and there were many people in the streets. Everyone wore fine clothes in beautiful, bright colours.

The wine-seller's daughter noticed a young *samurai* in the crowd. He was very handsome and she immediately fell in love with him. But before she could find out his name, he disappeared into the crowd. None of the other people in her party saw him. No one knew who he was.

Because she was in love, she remembered his face and his clothes very clearly. He wore a bright purple **robe**. In those days, the holiday robes of the young *samurai* were as colourful as the dresses of the young girls.

'If I wear a robe of the same colour,' she thought, 'perhaps he will notice me at the next holiday.'

So she ordered a bright purple robe with long arms. She loved it. She wore it every time she went out. When she was at home, she hung it in her room. She sat in front of it for hours and imagined the young *samurai* in it.

'Please let me win his love,' she prayed to the buddhas*: *'Namu myō hō rengé kyō!'*

She could think only of him. But she never saw him again. She fell ill, and died.

It was usual in those days to take the clothes of a dead person to the temple. And so the family took the purple robe to their temple and gave it to the priest.

The priest was able to sell the robe at a good price. It was an expensive robe, and the dead girl's tears did not show. A young lady bought it. She was about the same age as the dead girl. She only wore it for one day, then she fell ill and began to act strangely.

'The face of a beautiful young man is haunting me,' she cried. 'My love for him is killing me.'

And she died too; and the robe was given to the temple a second time.

---

* *shōgun:* Japanese warlords, 1192–1867
* buddha: a picture of the Buddha. (Siddhartha, 563–483 BC, started the Buddhist religion.)

robe /rəʊb/ (n) a long piece of clothing that covers your body

Again, the priest sold it. A third young lady bought it. She wore it only once before she fell ill. She talked of a beautiful shadow, and she died. The robe was given to the temple a third time.

'Should I sell it again?' thought the priest. But he did. Once more it was bought by a girl. Once more it was worn. And the girl fell ill and died. And the robe was given to the temple a fourth time.

Finally, the priest was sure that there were bad spirits in the robe. He told his assistants to make a fire in the temple garden.

They made a fire and threw the robe onto it. The robe began to burn. Suddenly, bright characters were seen on it. They were the characters of the girl's prayer: 'Namu myō hō rengé kyō!' One by one, the burning characters jumped out of the fire and onto the temple roof. The temple caught fire.

Pieces of burning wood fell onto the roofs of neighbouring houses. The street was soon on fire. A wind came up from the sea and made the fire stronger. The fire moved from street to street, and from area to area. It burned house after house, until it destroyed every building in the city.

That terrible day is still remembered in Tokyo. They call it the Day of the Great Fire of the Purple Robe.

The Travelling Priest and the Dead Body

*But then, in the deep silence of the night, a Shape came
into the room. It was very large and shadowy.*

M any years ago, there was a Buddhist priest called Musō Kokushi. He
travelled from place to place, performing religious acts. One day he was
walking alone through some mountains. He lost his way but there was no one to
ask for help.

'I'll have to sleep outside tonight,' Musō thought. But then, in the last light
from the sun, he saw a little hut on top of a hill. It was an *anjitsu**.

He hurried up the hill and found an old priest inside. Musō asked for a bed
for the night.

'There is no room here,' answered the old man roughly. 'But you will find
a small village in the next valley. Look down there. They will give you food and a
bed.'

Musō found his way to the little village. It had about twelve houses and
he was kindly received at the house of the headman. Musō was surprised to see
forty or fifty people in the main room of the house. But he was shown into a
small side room with a bed and some food.

* *anjitsu*: a hut for travelling priests

19

Musō was very tired and went to bed early, but at midnight he was woken by noises from the next room. It was the sound of loud crying. Then his door opened quietly and a young man came into the room. He carried a light.

'Excuse me, sir,' said the young man. 'I have some painful news. Yesterday I was the oldest son in this house. Today I am the head of the house. When you arrived this evening, you needed some rest. But now I must tell you what has happened. A few hours before you came, my father died. The people in the main room are all villagers. They have said goodbye to my father and left gifts of food for the buddhas. Now they are going to another village, about five kilometres away. None of us can stay in the village during the night after a death. We say our prayers, and then we go away. We leave the dead body alone.'

Musō was surprised.

'Strange things always happen in the house where the dead body lies,' the young man continued. 'Please come with us. We will find you a comfortable bed in the next village. But perhaps, as you are a priest, you are not afraid of bad spirits. You are very welcome to stay in this poor house.'

Musō answered, 'Thank you for your kind thoughts. I am sorry that I did not know about your father's death. I was tired, but I am a priest. It is my job to

say prayers for the dead. I will say prayers after you have gone. I will stay by the body until morning. I am not afraid of bad spirits or ghosts. Please do not worry about me.'

The young man was very happy with this answer. The rest of the family then came to thank him.

'Now, sir,' said the head of the house. 'We must go. We are sorry to leave you alone. But by the rule of our village, none of us can stay here after midnight. Please be careful while we are not here. If you see anything strange, tell us about it in the morning.'

Everyone left the house, except the priest. Musō went to the room where the dead body lay. A small Buddhist light burned in the room. Musō said prayers and then sat quietly for a few hours. There was no sound in the empty village.

But then, in the deep silence of the night, a Shape came into the room. It was very large and shadowy. Musō could not move or speak. As he watched, the Shape lifted the body. Then it ate it. It began at the head and ate everything, even the hair and the feet. Next, it ate all the gifts of food. And then the Shape went away.

When the villagers returned the next morning, they found the priest at the door of the house. They went into the main room. No one was surprised that the body and the gifts of food were not there.

But the head of the house said to Musō, 'Sir, you have probably seen unpleasant things during the night. We were all worried about you. We are happy that you are alive and well. We could not stay. If this law of the village is broken, terrible things will happen. When we follow the law, the body and the gifts disappear. Perhaps you saw what happened?'

Musō described the frightening Shape in the Death Room.

The villagers were not surprised, and the head of the house said, 'This is what the old stories tell us.'

'Does the priest on the hill sometimes come down and perform prayers for you?' asked Musō.

'What priest?' asked the young man.

'The old priest in the *anjitsu* on the hill. He refused to give me a bed when I first arrived. He sent me here to you.'

The listeners looked very surprised. After a short silence, the young man spoke again. 'Sir, there is no priest and there is no *anjitsu* on the hill. There has been no priest in this area for many years.'

Musō said nothing more on the subject. The headman and the villagers clearly did not believe him. But they were very polite and they did not say anything.

After Musō said goodbye to the villagers, he looked for the *anjitsu*. He found it easily and, this time, the old priest invited him inside.

'I am very sorry, very sorry!' cried the old priest. 'I am not pleased with myself.'

'You did not have to give me a room,' said Musō. 'You sent me to the village and they were very kind to me. I thank you for that.'

'I cannot give a room to *any* man,' said the priest. 'I am not thinking of that. I am sorry that you saw my real shape. *I* ate the dead body and the gifts last night before your eyes … I am a *jikininki**. Please listen to my terrible story.

'A long, long time ago I was a priest in this wild land. There was no other priest in the area. When mountain people died at that time, their bodies were brought here to me. Sometimes they came a very long way. I said prayers over their bodies but I was not a good priest. I thought only of the gifts of food and clothes that people gave me. And then I died … and I was born again as a *jikininki*.

* *jikininki*: a living thing that must eat people

'Since then, I have had to eat dead bodies. Every time a person dies in this area, I must eat them.

'Now, sir, do one thing for me. You are a priest. Please say prayers for me. Your prayers will help me to escape from this terrible life ...'

As the old priest said these words, he disappeared. The *anjitsu* disappeared too. And Musō Kokushi was left alone in the tall grass, on his knees. Near him was an old stone, half hidden by thick plants. It seemed to have the name of a priest on it.

3.1 Were you right?

Look back at Activity 2.4. Then put the right words in the sentences below.

> a cup and a stone   a snowstorm   a pot of gold
> a Japanese *samurai*   the broken cup

1 .... becomes a fortune-teller.

2 The Chinese fortune-teller owns only ....

3 The Chinese characters on .... bring Shōko Setsu

....

4 .... kills the old Japanese fortune-teller.

3.2 What more did you learn?

1 **Circle the best words to complete these sentences about the other stories.**

a Before the priest burns the purple robe, *three / four* girls die.

b In the story of the purple robe, a girl's love *is not as strong as money / can destroy a city.*

c The old priest in the *anjitsu welcomes Musō / sends Musō away.*

d Just before *Musō* arrives in the village, *the headman dies / the villagers all leave.*

e While the Shape is eating the dead body, Musō *is unable to move / tries to stop it.*

f The old priest was born again as a *jikininki* because he *was a selfish priest / lived in a wild land.*

2 **Discuss what has just happened.**

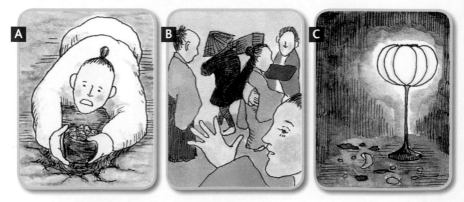

Language in use

Look at the sentence on the right. Then complete these first conditional sentences. Use the verbs that are given.

> 'If I **wear** a robe of the same colour, perhaps he **will notice** me.'

1   If the animal ....doesn't run over.... (not run over) Shōko Setsu's face,

   Shōko .... (not find) the gold.

2   If the fortune-teller .... (see) his future, he

   .... (not take) the mountain road.

3   Another girl .... (die) if the priest

   .... (sell) the robe again.

4   If the priest .... (burn) the robe, the people in the

   city .... (die).

5   Terrible things .... (happen) if the villagers

   .... (stay) with the dead body.

6   The old priest .... (escape) if Musō

   .... (say) prayers for the *jikininki*.

What happens next?

Look at the pictures in the next three stories. What do you think? Answer these questions.

1   (page 30) What kind of world has the young man gone to in his dream?

   ....

2   Will his dream end well or badly?

   ....

3   (page 32) Does the ghost want to frighten the child? What does she want?

   ....

4   (page 35) Why has a *samurai* cut this man's head off, do you think?

   ....

5   How did the man feel just before he died?

   ....

Miyata's Dream

They all greeted Miyata as he took his place opposite the king's daughter.
She was lovely, and her robes were as beautiful as a summer sky.

I n Toïchi there lived a soldier-farmer called Miyata Akinosuké. He was a rich and important man.

In Miyata's garden there was a beautiful old tree. He loved to rest under it on hot days. One very warm afternoon, he was sitting under this tree talking to two of his friends. They were drinking wine when suddenly he felt very sleepy.

'You must forgive me, my friends. I have to close my eyes for a few minutes,' said Miyata. And he lay down at the foot of the tree and began to dream.

In his dream he was lying in his garden. He saw a great line of people. He watched as they came down a hill.

'What fine and important people!' he thought, standing up. 'And they are coming towards my house!'

When they reached Miyata's house, a richly dressed man stepped out from the line.

'Good sir, you see in front of you a *kerai**,' said the man. 'Greetings from my lord, the King of the Spirits. He invites you to his palace. Please follow me on this fine horse.'

Miyata was very surprised by what was happening. He was unable to speak, but he climbed onto the horse and the journey began.

In a short time, everybody stopped in front of a very tall gateway. This gate was very close to Miyata's house, but he did not know it.

'I will tell the king that you are here,' said the *kerai*.

Miyata waited. Two men in purple robes and tall hats came from the gateway. They helped him get off the horse. Then they guided him through the gateway and across a large garden. The palace lay in front of them.

'I have never seen a building as wonderful and large as this,' thought Miyata. 'I cannot see the end of it either to the east or the west.'

His guides took him through the palace entrance into a wonderful room.

* *kerai*: someone who worked for an important person, like a king

27

They took him to a fine chair. Young girls in beautiful robes brought food and drink for Miyata.

Then the two guides stood in front of him.

'We must now tell you the reason for your visit here,' said one of the guides. 'Our lord, the king, has a request. He wants you to marry his daughter, the princess. Please follow us and we will take you to the king. He is waiting to receive you.'

'But first,' said the second guide, 'you must change your clothes.'

There was a large, gold-coloured box in the room. Inside were rich robes. The guides dressed Miyata in the robes and he looked like a prince. Then they took him to the King of the Spirits. The king wore a tall black hat and a yellow robe and sat above the others. To his left and right were many lords and ladies. They all wore beautiful clothes. Nobody moved.

Miyata greeted the king very politely.

'You have already been told the reason for this visit. I have decided that you will be my son. The wedding will now begin.'

Music filled the air. A long line of beautiful ladies came into the room. They took Miyata to the great room where his future wife waited. There he saw thousands of wedding guests. They all greeted Miyata as he took his place opposite the king's daughter. She was lovely, and her robes were as beautiful as a summer sky.

After the marriage, Miyata and the princess were taken to their rooms in another part of the palace. There they received many kind messages and wedding gifts.

Some days later, Miyata was called to the king.

'In the south-west part of our land there is an island called Raishu. You are now the lord of that island. You will find the people there friendly and helpful, but their laws are not yet the same as ours. Go there and make good laws for them. Be kind but strong. I have already made the preparations for your journey.'

Miyata was a good lord. For the first three years he made laws. After that, he did not have much to do. The people were healthy. The land was good. Nobody ever broke the laws. He lived happily for twenty more years. He and his wife had five sons and two daughters.

But in the twenty-fourth year of his stay, his good fortune came to an end. His wife fell sick and died. Her body was put under the earth on top of a beautiful hill – the mountain of Hanryoko. A beautiful stone in the shape of a Buddha was placed over her. But Miyata was very sad; he could not imagine life without her.

Some weeks later, a messenger arrived from the king.

'The king is very sorry for the death of your wife. This is the king's message: "We will now send you back to your own people and country. Your seven children are the grandchildren of the king and they will stay here. We will look after them well. Do not worry about them."'

Miyata prepared to leave. Then he was taken to the island's port. There, he said goodbye to the islanders and thanked his assistants. It took many hours. Then he went on to the beautiful ship that waited for him. The ship sailed out into the blue sea, under the blue sky ... the shape of the island of Raishu turned blue, and then grey and then disappeared ... and Miyata suddenly woke up – under the beautiful old tree in his garden!

For a minute, he did not know where he was. But then he saw his two friends. They were still drinking and talking happily.

'How strange!' he cried.

'Miyata was dreaming,' one of them laughed. 'What did you see, Miyata, that was strange?'

Then he told them his dream – his dream of twenty-four years in the Land of the Spirits ... on the island of Raishu.

'But you only slept for a few minutes!' said one friend.

'You saw strange things,' said the other friend. 'We also saw something strange while you slept. A yellow **butterfly** flew around your face; we watched it. Then it landed on the ground next to you, close to the tree. As soon as it landed, a very big **ant** came out of a hole. It pulled the butterfly down into the hole. A second before you woke up, the butterfly came out of the hole again. It flew about over your face. And then it disappeared. We do not know where it went.'

'Perhaps it was Miyata's spirit,' said the first friend. 'I thought it flew into his mouth ... But that does not explain his dream.'

'Maybe the ants can explain it,' said the other friend. 'Ants are strange things – possibly bad spirits ... Look! There is an anthill under the old tree ...'

'Let's look!' cried Miyata.

They used their hands to uncover the anthill. They were surprised by what they found.

'This is an ant city!' said Miyata. There were little roads and many holes. In one very big hole, much bigger than the rest, was a big yellow ant with a long black head. Thousands of little ants were all around it. They were looking after it.

butterfly /ˈbʌtəflaɪ/ (n) a small animal, often beautifully coloured. *Butterflies* have six legs and *fly*.

ant /ænt/ (n) a very small black or red animal with six legs; thousands of them live together in an *anthill*.

'There is the king!' cried Miyata, 'and this is his palace. Raishu is to the south-west … to the left of that big rock … Yes! Here it is! … How very strange! Now I am sure I can find the mountain of Hanryoko …'

He searched and searched. At last he discovered a little pile of earth. On top of it was a small stone. It looked like a Buddha. He picked up the stone, and below it he found … the dead body of a female ant.

A Dead Secret

*And she returned on the following night, and the night after that,
and every night – and the house became a house of fear.*

A long time ago, a rich man, Inamuraya Gensuke, lived in a part of country called Tamba. He had a daughter called O-Sono. As she was very pretty and clever, he decided to send her to a school in the city. He had a low opinion of country teaching, so he sent her to Kyoto.

After that, she married a friend of her father's family – a man called Nagaraya. She lived happily with him for nearly four years. They had one child – a boy. But O-Sono fell ill and died in the fourth year after her marriage.

O-Sono's body was placed in the ground and her husband was very sad. But the next night, her little son called his father.

'Mother has come back,' he shouted. 'She is in her bedroom.'

The family ran upstairs to O-Sono's old room. There they saw the ghost of the dead mother. She stood next to the box where she kept her clothes and personal things. They could see her head and shoulders clearly. But her legs and feet were shadowy.

They were afraid, and they left the room. Downstairs they discussed the matter.

'Women like their small things,' said the mother of O-Sono's husband. 'Perhaps O-Sono has come back to look at them. Many dead people do that. We should give her things to the temple. If we give her robes to the priest, her spirit can rest.'

The next morning, they emptied the box and took everything to the temple. But the next night, O-Sono came back. She looked at the box again. And she returned on the following night, and the night after that, and every night – and the house became a house of fear.

The mother of O-Sono's husband then went to the temple. She told the chief priest what was happening. Then she asked for help. The head priest was a clever old man. His name was Daigen Osho.

'She is worried about something in or near the box,' he said.

'But we emptied the box,' replied the old woman. 'There is nothing in the box.'

'Well,' said Daigen Osho, 'tonight I will come to your house. I will spend the night in the room and watch. No one must come into the room while I am there.'

After the sun went down, Daigen Osho arrived at the house. The room was ready for him. He stayed there alone and read Buddhist prayers. Nothing happened until after one o'clock. Then the ghost of O-Sono was suddenly in the room. She stood in front of the box. Her face was worried and she kept her eyes on the box.

The priest said a prayer and then spoke to the ghost of O-Sono.

'I have come here to help you. Perhaps there is something in that box that worries you. Shall I try to find it for you?'

The ghost seemed to move her head up and down.

The priest opened each part of the box. He searched carefully. He found nothing – there was only a sheet of pretty paper in each part. But the ghost continued to look at the box.

'What does she want?' thought the priest. 'I know! Perhaps there is something *under* the paper in one part of the box. He lifted the paper in the top part – nothing! He took out the paper in the next two parts – still nothing. But under the paper in the last part of the box he found … a letter!

'Does this trouble you?' he asked.

The shadowy ghost turned to him. Her eyes looked at the letter.

'Shall I burn it?' he asked.

Again, the ghost seemed to move her head a little.

'I will burn it in the temple this morning,' he promised, 'and no one will read it, except me.'

The ghost smiled and disappeared.

The sun was coming up when the priest came downstairs. The family waited below.

'Do not worry,' he said to them. 'She will not come back again.' And he was right.

The letter was burned. It was a love letter. It was written to O-Sono at the time of her studies in Kyoto. But only the priest knew what it said. The secret died with him.

You Can't Trick a Samurai

For the next few months, the assistants lived in fear.
They waited for a visit from the dead man's ghost.

The man was taken to the garden of a *yashiki**. His arms were tied behind his back. He was guided to a big sandy area, with stepping stones across it. The man was pushed down onto his knees. Assistants brought rice bags filled with small stones. They put the rice bags around the man so he could not move. Then they called the *samurai* to the garden. Everything was ready for him.

Suddenly the man cried out, 'Good sir, I did this crime but I am not a criminal. I only did it because I am stupid. I could not help it. I was born stupid. But that is not a crime. If you kill me for my stupidity, then that *is* a crime. After I die, my ghost will come back to earth. It will haunt you.'

The *samurai* knew what the man meant. Sometimes a person is angry when they are killed. Then their ghost can haunt the killer.

The *samurai* replied calmly, 'You may frighten us as much as you please – after your death. Will you give us a sign after we cut off your head?'

'Yes, I will,' answered the man angrily.

'Very well,' said the *samurai*. 'I am now going to cut off your head. In front of you there is a stepping stone. After your head is cut off, try to bite the stepping stone. That will be a sign that your ghost is angry with us … Then we will be frightened … . Will you try to bite the stone?'

'I will bite it!' cried the man, very angrily. 'I will bite it! I will bite …'

Sharp metal cut first through the air and then the man's neck. His body fell onto the rice bags. Blood shot into the air from his neck. His head **bounce**d onto the sand towards a stepping stone. Then suddenly, it caught the stone in its teeth. It held on tightly for a second and then fell back onto the sand. It did not move again.

No one spoke. The assistants were very frightened and looked at the *samurai*, but he was not worried.

For the next few months, the assistants lived in fear. They waited for a visit from the dead man's ghost. They saw many things that did not really exist. They were afraid of the wind in the trees. They were afraid of the shadows in the garden. At last they decided to speak to the *samurai*.

'Sir,' they said, 'please ask a priest to come here. He can say prayers and protect us from this dead man's spirit.'

---

* *yashiki*: a very large Japanese house

bounce /baʊns/ (v) to go up and down on the floor like a ball

'That is quite unnecessary,' said the *samurai*. 'I understand why you are afraid. The dying man wanted to frighten us. But there is nothing to fear.'

The assistants did not look happy.

'The reason is simple,' continued the *samurai*. 'Only the very last thought of a dying man is dangerous. I told him to bite the stone as a sign. His last thought when he died was, "I must bite the stone." It was not, "I must come back and haunt these people." He bit the stone. But he had to forget about haunting us. So, you see … there is nothing to worry about.'

The dead man gave no trouble. Nothing at all happened. You can't **trick** a *samurai* … but a *samurai* can trick you!

trick /trɪk/ (v/n) a clever way to do something that does not seem possible

4.1 Were you right?

Look back at Activity 3.4. Then complete these sentences.

At the end of Miyata's dream, his ....
dies. He leaves his seven children and returns to his
own ....

The .... wants to protect the
good name of herself, her .... and her
....

The .... is very angry and
the .... is very amused.

4.2 What more did you learn?

1 Draw lines to make sentences.

1	Nobody disagrees with the king in	a	the box.
2	Miyata's spirit was in	b	Kyoto.
3	Miyata lives through twenty-four years in	c	the stone.
4	O-Sono falls in love in	d	the land of the spirits.
5	O-Sono's love letter is in	e	his dream.
6	The *samurai* tricks	f	the yellow butterfly.
7	As he dies, the criminal bites	g	the criminal.

2 Describe a clever trick that someone has played on you.

....

....

Language in use

Look at this sentence. Then use present or past passive forms of the verbs in the sentences below.

> The man **was pushed** onto his knees.

1   The king sends Miyata to the island of Raishu.

Miyata .... to the island of Raishu by the king.

2   A very big ant pulls the yellow butterfly into a hole.

The yellow butterfly .... into a hole by a very big ant.

3   O-Sono hid the letter in the box.

The letter .... in the box.

4   O-Sono's ghost frightened the child when it returned for the letter.

The child .... by O-Sono's ghost when it returned for the letter.

5   They tied the man's arms behind his back.

The man's arms .... behind his back.

6   The *samurai* cut off the man's head.

The man's head .... by the *samurai*.

.4 What happens next?

Look at the new word at the bottom of page 38.

1   What (✓) do you think is happening in the picture on pages 40–41?

a ☐ The villagers are trying to ring the bell.

b ☐ The villagers are trying to steal the bell.

2   What do you think is happening in the picture on page 44?

a ☐ The woman in white is giving life to the old woodcutter.

b ☐ The woman in white is bringing death into the old woodcutter.

The Mirror and the Bell

They rang the bell as hard as they could. But it was a strong bell and nobody could break it.

Eight hundred years ago, the priests of Mugenyama in Totomi wanted a big **bell** for their temple. They needed metal. They asked local women to give their old metal mirrors to the temple. These could be used to make the bell.

Many women brought their mirrors to the temple, but one young woman soon began to miss her mirror very badly. She remembered her mother's stories about it. She remembered that it belonged to her grandmother before her mother. She remembered her own happy smiles in it.

'If I offer the priests enough money, I can buy it back,' she thought. 'But I do not have enough money,' she remembered. Her husband was a farmer, and they were not rich.

bell /bel/ (n) something that is rung in churches. *Bells* call people to prayer.

Every time she went to the temple, she saw her mirror. It lay on top of a pile of mirrors. She knew that it was her mirror. It had pictures of trees and flowers on the back.

'I have always loved those pictures,' she remembered. 'My mother first showed them to me when I was a baby.'

She wanted to steal the mirror and hide it.

'Then I will always keep it safe,' she thought. But she could see no way to steal it.

She became very unhappy. 'I feel I have given away part of my life,' she thought. 'People say that a mirror is the spirit of a woman. They are right.'

All the mirrors for the Mugenyama bell were sent to the bell-makers. They heated all the mirrors and turned them into hot metal – all except one mirror. Again and again, they tried to heat it, but it stayed cold. The mirror stayed a mirror.

They understood the reason. The owner wanted the mirror back. She did not give her gift with all her heart; her selfish spirit stayed in the mirror, and the mirror stayed hard and cold.

Of course, everybody heard about the matter. And, of course, everybody soon knew the owner's name. The woman was very sorry but very angry at the same time. She wrote a short letter:

'When I am dead, it will be easy to heat the mirror. Then you can use it for the bell. Ring the bell hard! If someone can break the bell, my ghost will return with a gift of money.'

And then she jumped in the river.

When an angry person kills herself, her final promise always comes true. That is what people say.

The dead woman's mirror was added to the bell metal and the bell was made at last. They named it the Bell of Mugen. People did not forget about the

dead woman's letter. As soon as the bell was hanging in the temple, everybody wanted to ring it. They rang the bell as hard as they could. But it was a strong bell and nobody could break it.

The people did not give up. Day after day, at all hours, they continued to ring the bell. The priests tried to stop them, but nobody listened to the priests. They probably could not hear them. The noise became impossible and the priests decided to act. They took the bell down and pushed it down the hillside into the river. The river was deep and the bell disappeared. And that was the end of it. Only the story was left.

There is an old Japanese idea called 'nazoraeru'. You *imagine* one thing but *do* another thing. This is almost the same as *doing* the first thing. Here is an example. You do not have enough money to build a Buddhist temple, but you *can* place a small stone in front of a Buddha. When you have enough money, you will build the temple. Today, you will place the stone. But the Buddha will *think* you have built the temple.

Here is another example. You make a little man out of dried grass. The little man looks like a big man who you do not like. You stick sharp pieces of metal into the little man and hang him on a temple tree at midday. If the big man dies soon after that, in great pain, that is *nazoraeru*.

Let's return to the bell. After it disappeared in the river, nobody could break it by ringing it. But people tried *nazoraeru*. They found something similar to a bell, hit it and broke it. They hoped to please the spirit of the mirror owner. But there was no sign of her ghost.

One of these people was a woman called Umegae. She was the lover of a famous *samurai* called Kajiwara Kagesue, of the Heiké people. The pair were travelling together. One day, Kagesue found that he had no money. Umegae remembered the Bell of Mugen. She took a metal bowl. She imagined it was the bell. She hit it hard until it broke. At the same time, she cried out for three hundred pieces of gold. A rich stranger heard the hitting and crying. He discovered the story and liked it. He gave Umegae three hundred pieces of gold.

After that, when people heard about Umegae's bowl, they all tried the same trick. One of them was a farmer who lived near Mugenyama, by the river. He was a lazy farmer and he spent all his money on women and drink in the town. He used the earth in his garden to make a Bell of Mugen. He hit it hard with a stick and cried out for gold. The bell broke.

Suddenly, a woman in a white robe came out of the ground in front of him. She had long hair and she held a pot in her arms.

'I have come to answer your prayer,' she said. 'I have brought your gift. It is what you have earned. Take this pot.'

She put a heavy pot into his hands and disappeared.

The happy man hurried into his house and told his wife the good news. He put the pot down on the floor. Then they opened it together. And they found that it was filled, to the top, with …

But no! I cannot tell you what it was filled with.

The Woman in White

He put out his hand in the dark and touched Mosaku's face. It was as cold as ice!
Mosaku was dead ...

Two woodcutters lived in a village in the Musashi area. Their names were Mosaku and Minokichi. Mosaku was an old man, and his assistant Minokichi was a boy of eighteen.

Every morning, they went together to a forest about eight kilometres from their village. There they cut wood. Every evening, they brought it home and sold it.

On the way to that forest there was a wide river. A boat took people across the river and there was a boat station on each side. Many times a bridge was built at the crossing place, but each time the bridge was lost. When the storms came, the water carried the bridge away. The river there was very strong.

Mosaku and Minokichi were on their way home one evening. It was very cold and it started to snow hard. Soon they were in the middle of a great snowstorm. They came to the boat station, but the boatman wasn't there. His boat was on the other side of the river. It was not a good day for swimming, so the two men went into the boatman's hut.

'We are lucky to have a roof over us,' they said.

The hut was a small wooden building with a door and no window. There was only room for two men to lie down on the floor. There was no place to make a fire. The two men closed the door and lay down in the dark. They put their coats over them and at first they did not feel very cold.

'The storm will soon end,' said Mosaku, and he fell asleep.

But the storm did not end soon. The boy lay awake for a long time, listening. The wind screamed and the snow fell hard against the door. The river was wild and angry. It was a terrible storm, and the air was becoming colder and colder. And then Minokichi too fell asleep.

At some time during the night, snow fell on Minokichi's face and woke him. The door of the hut stood open. By the snow-light, he saw a woman in the room – a woman all in white. She was between the two men and her face was close to Mosaku's face. A bright white smoke came from her mouth. Then she turned to Minokichi. He tried to cry out, but he could make no sound.

The white woman moved closer to him until her face almost touched his face. She was very beautiful, but her eyes frightened him. For a short time she continued to look at him. Then she smiled and spoke softly.

'I wanted to do the same to you as to the old man. But I feel sorry for you because you are so young. You are a pretty boy, Minokichi, and I will not hurt you now. But if you ever tell anyone – even your own mother – about me, I will kill you. Remember what I say!'

With these words, she left the hut. He found that he could move again. He jumped up and looked outside. But the woman was not there, and the snow was falling into the hut. Minokichi pushed the door closed against the snow. The room was dark again.

He thought about the woman. Was he dreaming? Did he mistake the snow-light in the doorway for the shape of a woman? He was not sure and he called to Mosaku. The old man did not answer and Minokichi was frightened. He put out his hand in the dark and touched Mosaku's face. It was as cold as ice! Mosaku was dead …

By the time the sun came up, the storm was over. When the boatman returned to his station, he found the two men. Minokichi lay next to the frozen body of Mosaku.

Minokichi woke up and was taken home. He was ill for a long time after that terrible night. He was very frightened by the old man's death, but he said nothing about the woman in white. As soon as he was well again, he returned to work. He went every morning to the forest and came back each night with wood. His mother sold the wood the next day.

One evening the following winter, Minokichi was on his way home. A girl was travelling on the same road. She was tall and very good-looking. She answered Minokichi's greeting in a voice like a song bird. They walked together and began to talk.

'My name is O-Yuki,' said the girl. 'Both my parents died not long ago and I am on my way to Yedo. I have some poor relatives there – I hope they will find me some work.'

Minokichi liked this strange girl. She really was very pretty.

'Will you marry soon?' he asked her. 'Are you promised to anyone?'

'No,' she laughed. 'I am free. What about you?'

'I am very young,' he answered. 'I look after my old mother, and we have not discussed marriage for me yet.'

And they walked without speaking. But their conversation seemed to continue in silence. As the Japanese say, 'The eyes can say as much as the mouth.'

When they arrived at Minokichi's village, he invited O-Yuki to rest at his house. She felt shy, but she went with him. His mother welcomed her, and prepared a hot meal for them. Minokichi's mother was very pleased with O-Yuki and invited her to stay. And O-Yuki never went to Yedo at all. She stayed in the house, and she married Minokichi.

O-Yuki was a very good daughter. When Minokichi's mother died five years later, her last words to her son were about his wonderful wife. And as time passed, O-Yuki and Minokichi had ten children. The children were all handsome and had beautiful fair skin.

The country people, too, thought that O-Yuki was wonderful and very different from them. Most country women look old when they are still young, but not O-Yuki.

'O-Yuki looks as young and fresh as the day she arrived in the village,' they said. 'Even after ten children!' they answered.

One night when the children were in bed, O-Yuki was mending a shirt.

Minokichi watched her and said, 'I remember something strange that happened when I was eighteen. I saw somebody then who was as beautiful and pale as you. She was very like you.'

O-Yuki did not lift her eyes from her work.

'Tell me about her,' she said. 'Where did you see her?'

And Minokichi told her the story of that night in the boatman's hut. He told her about the woman in white and the silent death of old Mosaku.

'That was the only time I saw a woman as beautiful as you,' he said. 'Of course, she was a spirit and I was afraid of her. I was very frightened … but she was so pale! … I have never been sure – was it a dream or was she the Woman of the Snow?'

O-Yuki threw the shirt on the floor and jumped up. She brought her face next to Minokichi's and screamed, 'It was I – I – I! O-Yuki! And do you remember my words? I said, "But if you ever tell anyone – even your own mother – about me, I will kill you." That is what I said! I will not kill you because of those children in there.' She pointed into the next room. 'And now you will have to look after them very, very well. If you ever hurt them, I will come back. Then I will kill you!'

She screamed sadly and her voice became thin, like the wind. Her body turned into bright white smoke. The smoke went up to the roof and out of the smoke hole. And she was never seen again.

5.1 Were you right?

Look back at your answers to Activity 4.4. Then answer these questions.

1 Who want old metal mirrors? ....

2 Who wants her mirror back? ....

3 Who tries to break the bell? ....

4 Who gives Umegae three hundred pieces
of gold? ....

5 Who dies in the hut by the river? ....

6 Who is going to Yedo to look for work? ....

7 Who never seems to get a day older? ....

8 Who tells the story of the woman in white
to O-Yuki? ....

5.2 What more did you learn?

1 **Put these pictures in order. Write the numbers, 1–6.**

2 **The woman in the white robe gives the lazy farmer a big pot. Discuss what is
in the pot.**

Language in use

Look at the sentence on the right. Choose a verb from the box below to complete each sentence.

> 'We are **lucky to have** a roof over us,' they said.

to have	to cross	to hear	to see	to work	to have

1 It was impossible .... the river in the storm.

2 It was too dark .... in the hut.

3 Minokichi was too ill .... for a long time.

4 Minokichi's mother was pleased .... O-Yuki as a daughter.

5 It was wonderful .... a beautiful family.

6 O-Yuki was angry .... the story of the Woman of the Snow.

4 What happens next?

Read these lines from the next two stories and discuss the questions. What do you think?

'The Bouncing Heads'

The head of the woodcutter, with the other four heads just behind it, jumped at Kwairyō. But the strong priest was ready for them.

1 Why are the heads not with their bodies?

....

2 Why are they attacking the priest?

....

3 How is the priest going to defend himself?

....

'The Samurai and the Tree'

He had nothing in the world to love except his tree. And then one year, in the summer, the tree died.

4 Why is the samurai so lonely?

....

5 Why does he love his tree?

....

6 What will he do after the tree dies?

....

The Bouncing Heads

The five people of the house were sleeping there.
But by the light of the moon he saw … that they had no heads!

Nearly 500 years ago, there lived a boy called Isogai Takétsura. He was learning to be a *samurai* and he could fight better than his teachers. He grew into a very strong young man and he was an excellent soldier in all ways. He soon became a *samurai* for the great Lord Kikuji of Kyūshū. Isogai fought bravely in the Eikyō war, and Lord Kikuji was very pleased with him.

But then Lord Kikuji lost the war. Isogai and the other *samurai* had no work and nowhere to live. Isogai did not look for a new lord. His heart was with Lord Kikuji, and he preferred to give up the life of a *samurai*. So he cut off his hair and became a Buddhist priest. He took the Buddhist name of Kwairyō, travelled across the country and taught people Buddhist law. Each night, he slept in a different place.

But under his priest's clothes, Kwairyō still had the heart of a *samurai*. As a soldier, and now as a priest, he laughed at danger. He travelled in all weathers and in all seasons of the year. He taught in places where other priests refused to go. These were dangerous times. A traveller alone was never safe; even a priest was not safe.

During his first long journey, Kwairyō visited a part of the country called Kai. One day, his journey took him through some mountains. He was travelling along a lonely road when it began to get dark. Kwairyō did not pass any villages or houses, so he decided to spend the night under the stars. He found a nice, grassy place by the road and lay down. He liked to be uncomfortable, and a hard rock made a good bed for him. He lay his head on a pile of stones and was happy. His body was strong, and he never worried about rain or wind or snow.

Kwairyō was just falling asleep when a man came along the road. The man was carrying a big pile of wood. He stopped when he saw Kwairyō.

With surprise in his voice, he asked, 'What kind of man can you be, good sir? How can you lie down alone in a place like this? There are ghosts and spirits around here – lots of them. Aren't you afraid of ghostly things?'

'My friend,' smiled Kwairyō, 'I am only a priest. I have nothing and I need nothing. I am not at all afraid of ghosts or other bad spirits. And I like lonely places. They are good places to think. I usually sleep in the open air and I have learned not to worry about my life.'

'You must be a very brave man, sir,' said the woodcutter. 'This place has a bad name – a very bad name. Around here we say, "A sensible man does not look for danger." And this is a very dangerous place to sleep. My house is very poor and small, but please come home with me, sir. I have no food to offer you. But there is a roof, and you can sleep under it safely.'

Kwairyō liked the man and accepted his offer.

The woodcutter took Kwairyō along a narrow path, away from the main road and through mountain forest. It was a rough and dangerous path. Sometimes they went around very steep rocks. Sometimes they walked on wet stones between sharp rocks. At last they came to an open space at the top of the hill. The moon shone brightly above them and Kwairyō saw a small house. Lights from the windows welcomed them.

The woodcutter took Kwairyō to a hut at the back of the house. Water came to the hut along wooden pipes from a little stream. The two men washed their feet. There was a vegetable garden behind the hut and some tall trees. Behind the trees was a waterfall. The two men watched the water for a short time. It moved from side to side in the moonlight, like a long white robe.

Kwairyō came into the small house with his guide. He saw four people – two men and two women – warming their hands at a little fire in the main room. They greeted the priest. The priest was surprised. These people were poor and lived in the middle of nowhere, but they used the polite greetings of the upper classes.

'These are good people,' he thought. 'Someone has taught them well.' He turned to the woodcutter.

'From your very polite speech and very polite welcome,' he said, 'I guess you were not always a woodcutter! Perhaps in the past, you belonged to a higher class?'

The woodcutter smiled.

'Sir, you are right,' he answered. 'I now live as you see here. Before, I was an important person from an important family. But I loved women and wine too much and I destroyed my life. I thought only about myself, and many people died because of me. I ran away and hid for many years. I want now to build my family's name and future again. I do not know if I will succeed. But there is one thing I can do. I can help people who are poorer than me.'

Kwairyō was pleased with the woodcutter's words.

'My friend, I have seen many men like you,' he said. 'They too lived bad lives when they were young. But later they worked hard to repair their mistakes. I see that you have a good heart. I hope that you will have a better life in the future. Tonight I will pray for you.'

Kwairyō said goodnight to the people in the house, and the woodcutter showed him to a very small room with a bed. Everyone went to sleep except the priest. He said prayers and read until late. Then he opened a window in his room. The night was beautiful and there were no clouds in the sky. Moonlight came through the trees and made dark shadows on the garden. The noises of the night were loud and musical, and behind them was the sound of the water.

As the priest listened to the water, he began to feel thirsty. He remembered the wooden pipes behind the hut and decided to get a drink. He pushed open his door very quietly and went into the main room. The five people of the house were sleeping there. But by the light of the moon he saw … that they had no heads!

He could not believe his eyes!

'Someone has come in and killed them,' he thought. 'But there is no blood. The necks are not cut. No! This is a trick played by bad spirits …' He thought for a minute. 'Perhaps I have come into the house of a *rokuro-kubi**? I have read about them. They have strange red characters on the back of their necks. Their heads like to move away from their bodies. If you find the body of a *rokuro-kubi* without its head, you must move the body to another place. Then the head and neck can never be joined again. And when the head cannot find the body, it bounces three times on the floor. It bounces like a ball and is very frightened … and then it dies. If these are *rokuro-kubi,* they will want to hurt me. I must do what the book says.'

The priest pulled the woodcutter's body to the window by its feet. Then he pushed it out of the window. He went to the back door, but it was locked on the inside. He looked up. There was a hole in the roof for the smoke to get out. He guessed that the heads went out that way too. He unlocked the door and went into the garden. Slowly and silently, he walked towards the trees. He could hear voices. He moved through the shadows until he found a good hiding place.

Then, from behind a tree, he saw them! Five heads! They were bouncing about, and talking and laughing! They were eating flies and other things they found on the ground.

After a few minutes, the woodcutter's head spoke to the others.

'That priest,' he said, 'who came tonight. How lovely and fat his body is! After we eat him, our stomachs will feel very full! It was a mistake to talk to him. Now he is praying for me. I can't go near him while he prays. But it is nearly morning – perhaps he is asleep. One of you go to the house. See what the man is doing.'

Another head – the head of a young woman – bounced away to the house. After a few minutes it came back, looking very worried.

* *rokuro-kubi*: a kind of bad spirit

'The priest is not in the house,' it said. 'He has gone! But that is not the worst thing. He has taken the woodcutter's body. I do not know where it is!'

At these words, the head of the woodcutter became truly terrible. Its eyes opened wide. Its hair stood up straight. It showed its teeth. Then it cried out loudly and tears fell from its eyes.

'Since someone has moved my body, I can never join it again! Then I must die! ... And all because of that priest! Before I die, I will kill that priest! I will pull him to pieces! I will eat him! ... And there he is – behind that tree! See him? He is not so brave now, is he?'

The head of the woodcutter, with the other four heads just behind it, jumped at Kwairyō. But the strong priest was ready for them. He held a big stick in his hand; with that stick he hit each head hard. Four of them bounced away, but the woodcutter continued to attack him. The priest hit the head again and again. The head jumped at him again and again. And then it caught him by the arm of his robe.

Kwairyō took the head by its hair. He held it in one hand and hit it again and again with the stick in his other hand. It held tight. Then it gave a long scream and it did not move again. It was dead. But its teeth still held the robe; Kwairyō was one of the strongest men in Japan, but he could not open the teeth.

The head continued to hang from his robe. He went back to the house and found the four other *rokuro-kubi*. Their heads, covered in blood from the fight, were back on their necks.

When they saw him at the back door, they all screamed, 'The priest! The priest!'

They ran away, through the other door, out into the wood.

To the east the sky was getting lighter. It was nearly morning. Kwairyō knew that bad spirits could do nothing in daylight. He looked at the head on his robe. Its face was dirty with blood and earth. He turned it over and saw the red characters on the back of its neck. He laughed loudly.

'This will make a good present for my friends at home!'

He put his things together and continued his journey through the mountains.

Kwairyō walked and walked. Finally, he came to a town called Suwa in Shinano. He went slowly along the main street, with the head at his side. Children screamed and ran away. Mothers screamed and fell to the ground. Men pointed and shouted, 'Murderer!' Then the police came and took the priest to prison.

When they questioned Kwairyō, he smiled. He said nothing, so he spent the night in the prison. The next morning, he was brought in front of the local judges.

'Why are you proudly walking through our town with this head on your robe?' they asked. 'Why are you not trying to hide this terrible crime?'

Kwairyō said, 'Sirs, *I* did not hang this head on my robe. I am not a murderer. This is not the head of a man. It is the head of a bad spirit – a *rokuro-kubi*. If I ended the life of a terrible *rokuro-kubi*, I was only trying to save my own life.'

And he told them the story from the start. He laughed loudly again when he came to the part about the five heads in the trees.

But the judges did not laugh. They believed he was a criminal. They did not ask any more questions, but discussed his case for a few minutes.

'We must punish him with death immediately,' said one.

They all agreed except one very old man. He spoke now for the first time.

'Let us first look carefully at the head,' he said. 'The head will tell us if the priest is lying. Bring the head here.'

The head still held Kwairyō's robe in its teeth. The police took the robe from Kwairyō's shoulders and brought it to the judges. The old man turned it round and looked at it carefully. On the back of its neck, he found some strange red characters. He showed these to the other judges. He also showed them the bottom of the neck.

'This was not cut with a knife,' he said. 'The skin here is smooth.'

The other judges agreed. They did not know what to think.

'The priest's story is true,' the old man continued. 'This is the head of a *rokuro-kubi*. You always find these red characters on the back of the neck of a *rokuro-kubi*. Look! These letters are real – the priest has not painted them on. These *rokuro-kubi* have lived in the mountains of Kai since time began. But you, sir,' he said to Kwairyō, 'what kind of priest are you? You are braver than an ordinary priest – you are more like a soldier than a priest. Perhaps you belonged to the *samurai* class?'

'You have guessed correctly, sir,' replied Kwairyō. 'I was a *samurai* before I became a priest. In those days I was afraid of nothing and nobody. My name then was Isogai. You may remember it.'

'Ah!' cried voices in the courtroom.

Many of them knew the name Isogai. Suddenly, everyone was Kwairyō's friend and not his judge.

They took him to the house of the local lord. There the lord welcomed him and gave him a great meal. When Kwairyō left Suwa, he was as happy as a priest may be in this world. And the head? He took it with him. He planned to give it to a friend as a present from his great journey.

And this is what happened to the head …

A day or two after he left Suwa, Kwairyō met a robber. The robber stopped him in a lonely place and asked him to take off his robe. Kwairyō immediately took off the robe and gave it to the robber. The robber then saw the head. He was a brave robber, but he dropped the robe and jumped back.

'You! What kind of a priest are you?' he cried. 'You are a worse man than me. It is true that I have killed people … But I have never walked about with anybody's head on my robe. Well, sir, I would like to have that head. I can frighten people with it. Will you sell it to me? You can have my robe for your robe and this piece of silver for the head.'

'I will give you the head and the robe,' said the priest. 'But I must tell you that this is not the head of a man. It is the head of a *rokuro-kubi* and it will bring you trouble. Please remember that I told you to be careful.'

'What a nice priest you are,' said the robber. 'You kill men, and you joke about it! But I am not joking. Here is my robe. And here is the money. Now give me the head.'

'Take it,' said Kwairyō. 'I was not joking either. You are stupid enough to pay good money for a *rokuro-kubi*'s head. That is the only joke.'

And Kwairyō continued on his way.

So the robber got the head and the robe. For some time he used the head in his business and made plenty of money. But when he reached Suwa, he learned the real history of the head. And then he was afraid. He decided to take the head back to its body.

He found his way to the lonely little house in the mountains of Kai. But nobody was there and he could not find the woodcutter's body. He made a hole in the earth under the trees behind the garden. He put the head in the hole and covered it with earth. He put a stone over the hole. He found a priest to say some prayers for the spirit of the *rokuro-kubi*. And that stone – the Stone of the *Rokuro-kubi* – is still there today.

The Samurai and the Tree

'I am glad,' he said, but he was not really glad. His heart was full of pain. He loved the old tree too much.

I n Wakegori, in Iyo, there is a very old and very famous fruit tree. It is called 'The Fruit Tree of the Sixteenth Day', because every year its flowers open on the sixteenth day of the first month … and only on that day. It flowers in the Time of Great Cold. It is more natural for fruit trees to wait for the warm spring weather. But there is another life that brings that tree into flower. There is the ghost of a man in that fruit tree.

The ghost was a *samurai* of Iyo. The tree grew in his garden. It always flowered at the usual time – at the end of March or in the first days of April. He played under that tree when he was a child. His parents and grandparents, and their parents and grandparents, all played there too. For more than a hundred years, children hung pieces of brightly coloured paper from the tree. A beautiful poem was written on each piece of paper.

The man grew very old. All his children died before him. He had nothing in the world to love except his tree. And then one year, in the summer, the tree died.

The man was very sad. Nothing could make him smile. And then his kind neighbours bought him a young and beautiful fruit tree. They planted it in his garden. They hoped to see his smile.

He thanked them. 'I am glad,' he said, but he was not really glad. His heart was full of pain. He loved the old tree too much. Nothing could take its place.

And then he had a happy thought. It was the sixteenth day of the first month. He went alone into his garden and he spoke politely to the old, dead tree.

'Now please, dear tree,' he said, 'flower just once more. I am going to die in your place.' (Some people believe that one can give away one's life to another person, or to an animal, or even to a tree.)

He put a white cloth under the tree, and more white cloths on top of the first white cloth. And he sat down on the pile of cloths. And then he performed *hara-kiri** in the *samurai* way. His ghost went into the tree and it flowered immediately.

And every year the tree still flowers on the sixteenth day of the first month, in the season of snow.

---

* *hara-kiri*: the act of cutting open your own body and killing yourself

6.1 Were you right?

Look back at your answers in Activity 5.4. Then tick (✓) the information that is correct.

1 ☐ Kwairyō was once a priest called Isogai.
2 ☐ The woodcutter and his friends are *rokuro-kubi*.
3 ☐ They have red characters on the back of their hands.
4 ☐ Their heads can leave their bodies.
5 ☐ They eat flies.
6 ☐ The Fruit Tree of the Sixteenth Day flowers later than other fruit trees.
7 ☐ Iyo performs *hara-kiri* in front of the tree because it is dead.

6.2 What more did you learn?

Discuss what is going to happen next. Complete each sentence.

1 The woodcutter ... .

2 Kwairyō ... .

3 The bouncing heads ... .

2 The police ... .

Language in use

Look at the sentence on the right. Then choose one verb from each box for each sentence below. Use past continuous or past simple forms.

> Kwairyō **was travelling** along a lonely road when it **began** to get dark.

A   look for   bounce
fall asleep   bring   walk

B   see   find   notice
meet   come

1   Kwairyō .... when a man .... along the road.

2   Kwairyō .... a drink when he .... the five bodies without heads.

3   The heads .... in the trees when Kwairyō .... them.

4   Kwairyō .... away from Suwa when he .... a robber.

5   The old man's neighbours .... him some tea when they .... his dead body under the old tree.

4 What happens next?

Read these questions about the last stories and write your ideas.

1   A man meets a woman crying by the road. What is strange about her?
....

2   Then he meets a travelling food-seller. What is strange about him?
....

3   A hunter shoots one of a pair of birds. What will the other bird do?
....

4   Before a man's young wife dies, what does she ask him to promise?
....

5   A young man follows a wise priest up a mountain. There is no life on the mountain – no water, no plants, no birds. What is the mountain made of?
....

Mujina

He ran and ran up the hill. Everything around him was black and empty.
He ran and ran, and he did not look back.

On the Akasaka Road in Tokyo, there was a steep hill on one side of the road. At the bottom of the hill was a river. It was very wide and the water was deep. On the other side of the road were the high stone walls of a palace.

In the days before streetlights, this area was very lonely after dark. Nobody wanted to cross the hill alone. People believed that a *mujina** walked there.

The *mujina* was last seen there in about 1875. An old man from the Kyōbashi area of the city was hurrying home in the dark. He was late and he decided to cross the hill. But then he saw a woman sitting by the river. She was alone and crying wildly.

'Perhaps she is going to throw herself in,' he thought. So he went to help.

The woman was small and very well dressed. The man decided that she was from a good family.

'*O-jochū**!' he called, as he came near. '*O-jochū*, do not cry like that! Tell me what the trouble is. I will gladly help you if I can.'

He meant what he said; he was a very kind man.

But she continued to cry. She hid her face in her robe.

'*O-jochū*,' he said again, even more kindly. 'Please, please listen to me. This is no place for a young lady at night. Do not cry! How can I help you?'

She stood up slowly, but turned her back to him and continued to cry. She held the arm of her robe across her face.

He put his hand lightly on her shoulder.

'*O-jochū*! *O-jochū*! Listen to me, for just one minute ...'

But then that *O-jochū* turned round. She dropped the arm of her robe ... she put her hand to her face ... And the man saw that she had no eyes or nose or mouth. He screamed and ran away. He ran and ran up the hill. Everything around him was black and empty. He ran and ran, and he did not look back. At last he saw a light. The light was far away but he ran towards it. It was a travelling *soba**-seller, selling bowls of *soba* by the side of the road.

The old man from Kyōbashi was very pleased to see him and his light. He fell to the ground at the *soba*-man's feet.

'Aaah!!' he cried. He could not speak.

* *mujina*: a dog-like animal that can change its shape
* *O-jochū*: a polite Japanese name for a young lady that you do not know
* *soba*: a popular Japanese dish

'Hey!' said the *soba*-man. 'What is the matter with you? Has somebody hurt you?'

'No,' said the old man finally. 'Nobody has hurt me. Only …. Aaah!'

'Only frightened you?' said the man. He was not very friendly. 'Robbers?'

'No, not robbers,' said the old man. 'I saw … I saw a woman – by the river – and she showed me … aaah! I cannot tell you what she showed me!'

'Was it anything like this?' cried the *soba*-man, putting his hand to his own face.

As he spoke, his eyes, nose and mouth disappeared. Suddenly, his face became as smooth as an egg … And, at the same time, his light went out.

The Hungry Hunter

*'You do not know what you have done! But tomorrow,
go to Akanuma and you will see. You will see ...'*

S onjō was a **hunt**er who lived in Tamura-no-Go, in the area of Mutsu. One
day he went hunting, but he did not kill anything all day. On his way home,
he had to cross a river at a place called Akanuma. From the bridge, he saw two
*oshidori** swimming together in the water. It is not good to kill *oshidori*, but
Sonjō was very hungry and he really wanted to kill something. He shot at the
pair and killed the male. The female escaped into tall plants at the side of the
river and disappeared.

Sonjō took the dead bird home and cooked it.

That night, he dreamt a sad dream. A beautiful woman came into his room
and stood by his bed. She began to cry loudly. Sonjō's heart hurt as he listened.

'Stop!' cried Sonjō. 'You are pulling my heart out.'

'Why? Why did you kill him?' cried the woman. 'What did he ever do to
you? At Akanuma we were so happy together, and then you killed him. Do you
even know what you have done? You have killed me too. I will not live without
my husband. I came to tell you this.'

* *oshidori*: river birds

hunt /hʌnt/ (v) to look for and kill animals for food or sport

64

She cried more wildly now. Sonjō felt her pain deep inside himself. Then she said the words of a poem:

'When the sun went down
I invited him to return with me.
Now I sleep alone
In the shadows of the river
In Akanuma.
How deeply sad I am!'

She shouted to Sonjō, 'You do not know what you have done! But tomorrow, go to Akanuma and you will see. You will see …'

And she went away.

When Sonjō woke up the next morning, his dream seemed real. He remembered her words: 'Tomorrow, go to Akanuma and you will see.' He decided to go there immediately.

He came to the river at Akanuma. He saw the female *oshidori*, swimming alone. The bird saw Sonjō, but she did not try to escape. She swam straight towards him, looking right into his eyes. Then she moved her head down to her chest. She took a piece of skin in her mouth and suddenly pulled her body open. She performed *hara-kiri* in front of the hunter's eyes …

Sonjō shaved his head and became a priest.

The Promise

'Only the Buddhas know where we will meet. But I am sure that
I will come back to you. Remember my words …'

A long time ago, in the town of Niigata in Echizen, there lived a man called Nagao Chōsei.

Nagao was the son of a doctor, and he studied for the same profession. When he was very young, he was promised in marriage to a girl called O-Tei. She was the daughter of one of his father's friends.

'The wedding will be after Nagao finishes his studies,' agreed the families. 'O-Tei will be fifteen then, and that will be the perfect time.'

But O-Tei was not a healthy girl. When she was nearly fifteen, she became very ill. Death was near, and she sent for Nagao.

'Nagao, my love, our wedding will never happen. I am going to die. My body is weak. The Buddhas know what is best for us. I am happy to die now. Promise me that you will not cry for me. And I want to tell you something. I believe that we will meet again.'

'We will meet again,' said Nagao, 'and in that Perfect Land there will be no pain.'

'No, no,' she answered softly. 'I do not mean the Perfect Land. I believe we will meet again in this world.'

Nagao looked at her with wide eyes. She saw his surprise and she smiled.

She said in her dreamy voice, 'Yes, I mean in this world, in your own present life, Nagao. … of course, only if you want to. I will be born a girl again and grow up. You must wait fifteen years. That is a long time, but you are only nineteen years old …'

Nagao did not want to trouble her dying minutes.

'We are promised in marriage for seven lives,' he answered. 'I will wait.'

She looked closely at his face.

'You are not sure,' she said.

'My dear one,' he answered. 'How will I know you in another body with another name? You must give me a sign.'

'I cannot do that. Only the Buddhas know where we will meet. But I am sure that I will come back to you. Remember my words …'

She spoke no more, and her eyes closed. She was dead.

Nagao loved O-Tei deeply and he was very sad about her death. He wrote a promise on a piece of paper: 'I will marry you, O-Tei, if you return to me in another body.' And he put the promise in the ground with O-Tei's body.

But Nagao was an only child. His family wanted him to marry and they found another wife for him. After his marriage, he continued to visit O-Tei's stone. He placed gifts there for the Buddhas and he always remembered her with love. But over time, the picture of O-Tei in his mind was not so sharp. She was like a dream that is hard to remember. And the years passed.

During these years Nagao had many troubles. First his parents died, and then his wife and only child. So he found himself alone in the world. He left his home, with its sad memories, and began a long journey.

One day he arrived at Ikao, a mountain village famous for its water. The country was beautiful there. He found a place to stay in the village and a young girl brought his food and drink. As soon as he saw her, his heart jumped in his chest. She looked like O-Tei.

Nagao thought he was dreaming. The girl came and went, bringing fire and food. Everything about her brought back memories of O-Tei. He spoke to her and she replied in a soft, sweet voice.

'May I ask you a question?' he asked.

'Of course, sir,' she answered.

'You look very much like a person from my past. I was surprised when you first came into the room. Where do you come from and what is your name?'

Immediately, and in the voice of the dead, she answered, 'My name is O-Tei. You are Nagao, my promised husband. Seventeen years ago, I died in Niigata. You wrote a promise and put it in the earth with my body. And I came back …'

As she spoke these last words, she fell to the ground.

Nagao married her and the marriage was happy. But O-Tei never remembered her answer to Nagao on that day in Ikao. The memory of her earlier birth – remembered at the point of that meeting – was lost for ever.

The Mountain

The young man picked up one of these rocks. It was smooth but it was not a rock.
He looked at it and death smiled back at him.

They came to the foot of the mountain as the sun went down. There was no sign of life – no water, no plants, no birds in the sky. It was wild and empty. They looked up and the mountain, too, was wild and empty. The top was lost in the clouds.

Then the Bodhisattva* said to his young friend, 'I will show you what you want to see. But it is a long climb and the way is rough. Follow me and do not be afraid. You are strong.'

It quickly grew dark and there was no path. There was no sign of other men. It was a difficult climb over white rocks and stones. The rocks moved or turned with each step. Sometimes a pile of them suddenly bounced down the mountain, making a terrible, empty sound. And the dark of the night became deeper.

'Do not be afraid,' said the Bodhisattva. 'The way is hard but there is no danger.'

Under the stars they climbed – faster and faster. A spirit pushed them on. When they looked down, they saw a sea of cloud.

They could not see the rocks they stepped on. Sometimes the rocks broke. When this happened, a cold, white fire started. It quickly died.

The young man picked up one of these rocks. It was smooth but it was not a rock. He looked at it and death smiled back at him. They were not walking on rocks.

'Let's continue, my son,' said the teacher. 'We still have a long way to go.'

They climbed and climbed through the dark. They felt the soft, strange breakings under their feet. They saw the icy fires start and die.

And then the black of night turned grey. The stars began to disappear. They looked to the east and there was light.

They still climbed. The icy feel of death was around them – and the deepest silence. The sky in the east began to turn gold.

And the light shone on the mountain that they climbed. And the young man shook with fear. The ground was not ground. They were climbing over a mountain of **skull**s. Teeth and eye holes were everywhere.

* Bodhisattva: a Buddha who stays on earth. He stays here to help people.

skull /skʌl/ (n) the hard part inside your head

'Do not be afraid, my son!' cried the Bodhisattva. 'Only the strong of heart can see what you will see.'

Behind them, the world had disappeared. There were only clouds, and the sky above, and the skulls, going up and up for ever.

The sun climbed with the climbers, but the sun's light was not warm; it was sharp and cold. The journey was suddenly too much for the young man. He could not move his feet and he cried out.

'Hurry, hurry, my son,' cried the Bodhisattva. 'The day is short, and the top of the mountain is far away.'

But the boy screamed, 'I am afraid. This place is terrible! And I am too weak to continue.'

'You will be strong again, my son,' said the teacher. 'Look below you and above you and around you. What do you see?'

'I cannot look!' cried the boy. 'I cannot look below. Above and around me are the skulls of men.'

'But, my son,' said the Bodhisattva, laughing softly, 'you do not know what this mountain is made of.'

'I am frightened! There is nothing except the skulls of men.'

'A mountain of skulls it is,' replied the Bodhisattva. 'But, my son, they are all *your* skulls! Each one has at some time been the home of your dreams and needs. Not one of them belongs to another person. They have all been yours, in all your millions and millions of lives.'

1 **Lafcadio Hearn found the ghost stories in this book when he lived in Japan between 1890 and 1904.**

Work with another student. Read the notes for Student A or Student B, and cover the other student's information. Ask and answer questions to find out about Hearn's life.

Student A

1850	Lafcadio Hearn – born Lefkas, Greece – mother Greek
1856	?
1866	Accident at school – blind in left eye
1869	?
1875	Lost job at newspaper because married black woman (marriage didn't last)
1890	?
1891	Married daughter of samurai – took new name, Koizumi Yakumo
1903	?
1904	Died in Japan

Student B

1850	What happened in 1850?
1856	Father Irish – family moved to Dublin
1866	?
1869	Went to United States – got newspaper job, Cincinnati – reported on murder
1875	?
1890	Went to Japan for newspaper job – but became teacher
1891	?
1903	His book, 'Kwaidan: Stories and Studies of Strange Things', came out – most stories in this book from there
1904	?

2 **What is the most frightening thing that has ever happened to you? Tell other students about it.**

Complete this guide to the ghosts and spirits of Japan. What does each spirit look like? Where does it live? What does it do? How do you stop it?

A GUIDE TO JAPANESE GHOSTS AND SPIRITS

A jikininki

A jikininki

A mujina

A mujina

A rokuro-kubi

A rokuro-kubi

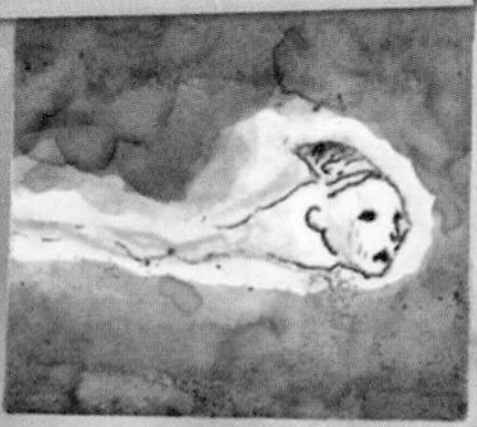

The Oni-bi

The Oni-bi

WORK IN SMALL GROUPS. YOUR GROUP IS GOING TO WRITE AND PERFORM A
TWO-MINUTE GHOST PLAY.

1 Which of these are important in a ghost story? Discuss the different ideas.
Decide which you are going to have in your story.

- ordinary people
- strange people
- a dark and mysterious theatre
- an ordinary room
- a slow beginning
- a lot of screaming and blood

- suggestions of murder or death, but off stage
- loud music
- clever and funny words
- very few words

2 Choose a ghostly place for your play.

3 Now choose the time of day and the weather.

Think of some people for the play, and a ghost. Write notes. Then decide which of you is going to play which person.

Person 1:

Name: Age: Sex:

Profession:

Believes in ghosts: Yes / No

Other notes:

Person 2:

Name: Age: Sex:

Profession:

Believes in ghosts: Yes / No

Other notes:

Person 3:

Name: Age: Sex:

Profession:

Believes in ghosts: Yes / No

Other notes:

Ghost(s):

Name before death:

Age: Sex:

Reason for haunting the living:

Discuss answers to these questions. Write notes.

a What has already happened? Why are these people in this place at this time?

....

....

b What is going to happen?

....

....

6 **Write your ghost play. Then practise it. Time it. Does it last two minutes?**

TITLE: _____

PLACE: _____

TIME OF DAY: _____

OTHER STAGE NOTES: _____

[WHO COMES IN?] _____

_____

_____

_____

_____

_____

_____

_____

_____

_____

_____

_____

_____

_____

_____

_____

_____

_____

_____

_____

_____

_____

_____

_____

_____

THE END

7 **Now perform your play for other students. Make it as frightening as you can.**